AUTUMN HARVEST
MICHAEL SCOTT

Project Manager: Dale Tucker
Art Design: Carmen Fortunato and Jorge Paredes

Michael Scott

Michael Scott has composed, arranged, and produced music for television, records, films, commercials, concerts, and print publishing. His versatile writing and producing skills have contributed to projects for Paramount Pictures, Johnny Carson Productions, Universal Studios, 20th Century Fox, MCA Records, NBC Television, Columbia Pictures, and Warner Bros. Publications, his current publisher. In addition, he has worked for such music industry figures as John Williams, Quincy Jones, Stevie Wonder, David Foster, Randy Newman, Carla Bley, and rock band Pink Floyd.

A lifelong supporter of music education, Michael has taught privately, lectured at colleges and conventions, conducted seminars and workshops with such music luminaries as Henry Mancini and Albert Harris, and contributed numerous compositions and arrangements to the educational print music field.

He is a member of BMI, the National Academy of Recording Arts and Sciences, the American Society of Music Arrangers and Composers, and the American Federation of Musicians.

Contents

OFF THE BEATEN PATH

By MICHAEL SCOTT

6

AUTUMN HARVEST

By MICHAEL SCOTT

Graceful and flowing ♩ = ca. 120

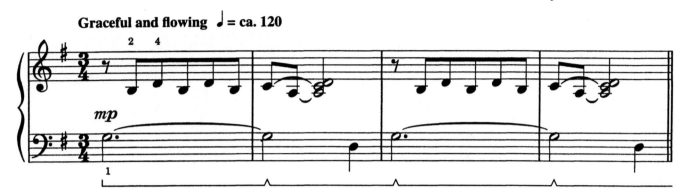

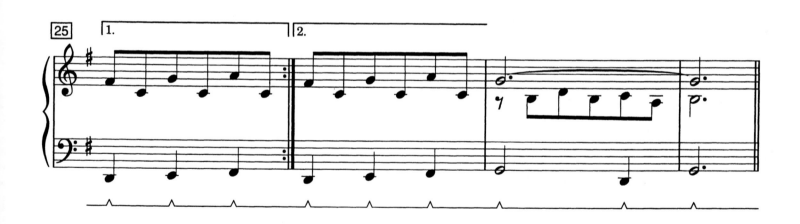

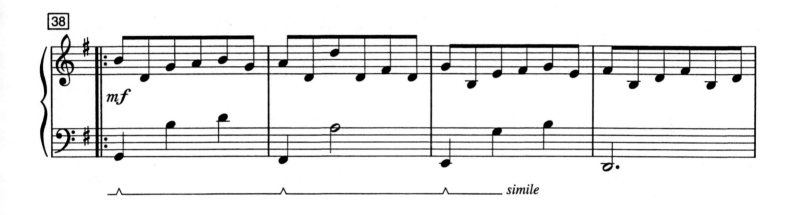

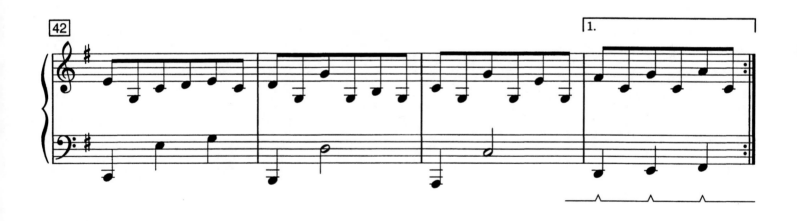

RAINFOREST

By MICHAEL SCOTT

*Notes in parentheses may be omitted.

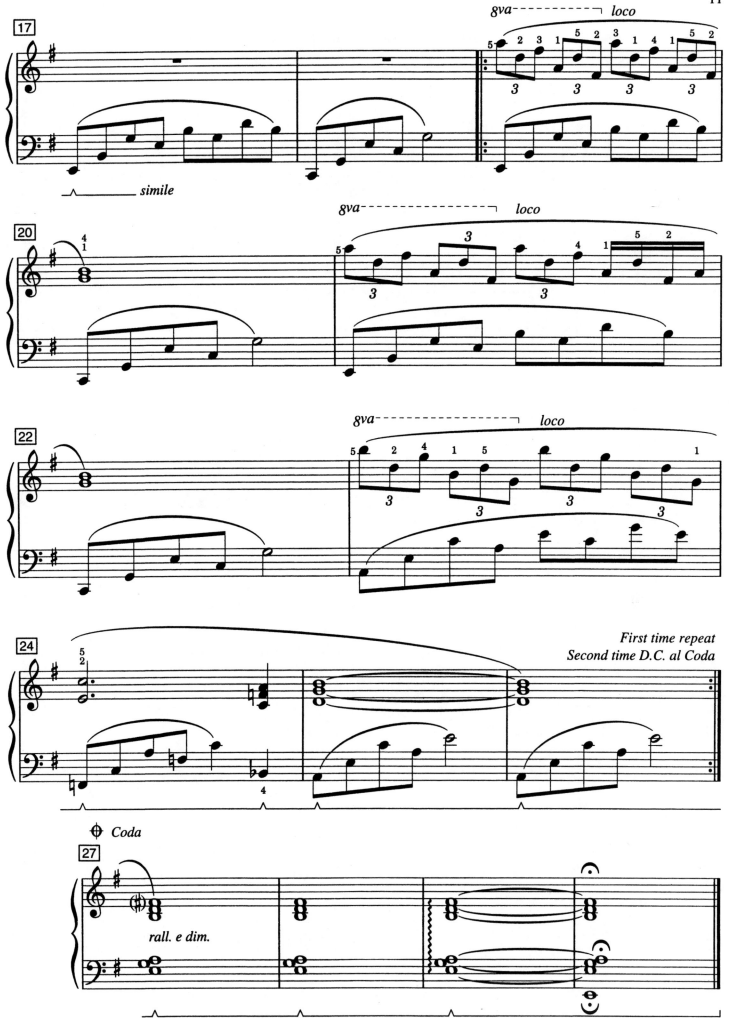

Dedicated to the memory of Corey Martin

THAT GRACE MAY ABOUND

Gently and somewhat freely ♩ = ca. 50

By MICHAEL SCOTT

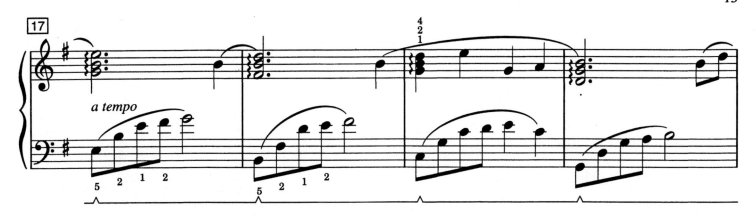

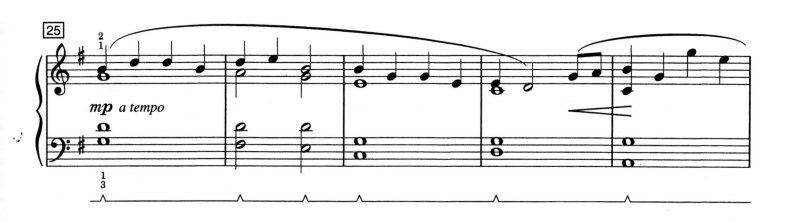

WANDERING DOWN THE LATITUDES

By MICHAEL SCOTT

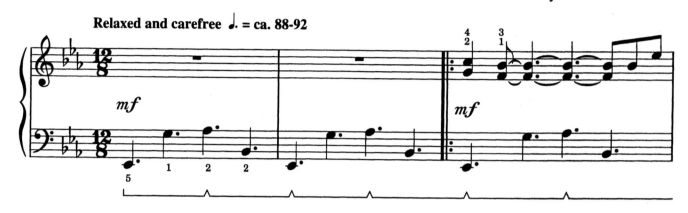

HAIKU

By MICHAEL SCOTT

*Pedal the grace notes so they sustain.

SPRING RIVER

By MICHAEL SCOTT

THE NEW WORLD*

By ANTONIN DVOŘÁK
Adapted and Arranged by MICHAEL SCOTT

*From *Symphony No. 5 in E minor, Op. 95* ("New World" Symphony)